BIBLE TEACHING SHEETS: THE NEW TESTAMENT
NIV EDITION

ISBN: 978-1-953489-16-6

©2020 Wildrose Media. USA.

All rights reserved. No part of this publication may be reproduced, distributed or transmitted in any form or by any means without prior written permission of the publisher except in the case of brief quotations for critical reviews and certain other noncommercial uses permitted by copyright law.

www.wildrose-media.com

Sermon Notebook Journal for Kids ages 9-12
ISBN: 978-1-953489-10-4
ISBN: 978-1-953489-13-5

AVAILABLE ON AMAZON

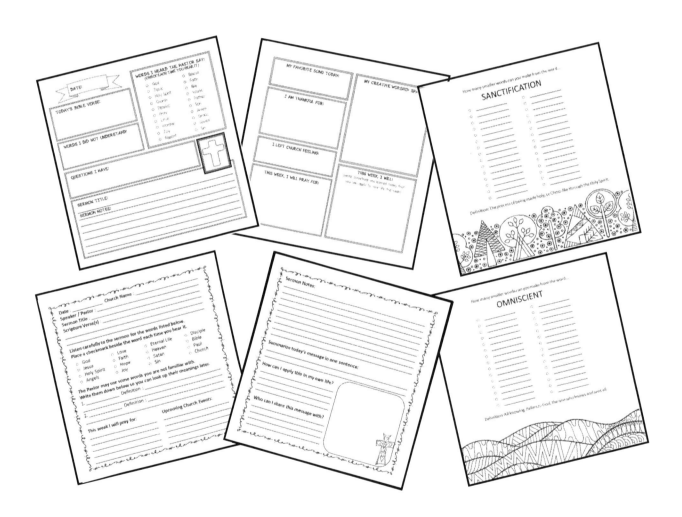

www.wildrose-media.com

BIBLE TEACHING SHEETS: THE NEW TESTAMENT
NIV EDITION

MATTHEW

Literary Style: Gospel, Historical Narrative

New Testament Book #: 1
# of chapters: 28

Author: Attributed to Matthew, called Levi in the gospels of Mark and Luke. One of Jesus' twelve apostles. A Jewish tax collector prior to following Jesus, he was an eyewitness to many of the events described.

Audience: Written primarily to the Jewish people who had converted to Christianity. Matthew contains over 50 Old Testament prophecies which the Jews were familiar with.

Setting: Bethlehem, Nazareth, Galilee and Judea. Events recorded in Matthew took place from about 5 BC to AD 33, Jesus' lifetime.

Of Interest: Called the "Gateway to the New Testament". Probably written between AD 60-70, before the fall of Jerusalem.

General Information about the book of MATTHEW:

Matthew begins with a genealogy, a list of the ancestors of Jesus Christ. The purpose of this list of names was to link Jesus to the lineage of both Abraham and King David, the fulfillment of Old Testament prophecy. It includes women and non-Jewish people (Rahab, Ruth) to show Jesus came for ALL, not just the Jews. Matthew shows Jesus as:
- a new Abraham, Jesus is head of a new nation which includes both Jews and Gentiles.
- a new Moses- the deliverer, teacher, law giver, and mediator between God and His people.

Content Highlights:
- Genealogy of Jesus
- An angel appears to Joseph, the birth of Jesus Christ, visit of the Magi, flight into Egypt
- Baptism of Jesus, temptation in the desert
- Jesus' earthly ministry – calls and instructs His disciples, parables, miracles, teachings
- The transfiguration
- Signs of the end times, the last days
- Jesus' final week, the Lord's Supper
- Jesus' arrest, crucifixion, burial, and resurrection
- The Great Commission

Note:
- The Beatitudes (chapter 5:1-12)
- The Lord's Prayer (chapter 6:9-15)
- Matthew is the only gospel to record the slaughter of the innocents by order of King Herod (chapter 2).

Therefore go and make disciples of all nations, baptizing them in the name of the Father and of the Son and of the Holy Spirit.
Matthew 28:19 NIV

KEY Verses:
- 3:1-3
- 5:1-12
- 5:13-16
- 5:17-18
- 6:19-21
- 6:33-34
- 7:7-8
- 10:1-16
- 12:36-37
- 16:13-19
- 16:24-27
- 20:36-28
- 24:4-14
- 28:5-6
- 28:18-20

Theme: Jesus Christ is the King, the promised Messiah who came for both Jews and Gentiles to restore God's kingdom on earth.

MARK

Literary Style: Gospel, Historical Narrative

New Testament Book # **2** # of chapters **16**

Author: Mark, also called John Mark, was a disciple of Peter's and cousin to Barnabus. The church in Jerusalem gathered at his mother's house. He accompanied Paul and Barnabus on part of their first missionary trip.

Audience: Written to Gentile Christians living in Rome. Mark was likely written between AD 55-59 and is considered the first of the three synoptic gospels.

Setting: Galilee and Jerusalem. Events recorded in Mark took place during Jesus' earthly ministry, from about AD 30-33.

Of Interest: Some translations include an extended ending (chapter 16:9-20) - the great commission and ascension. Earlier versions end at 16:8, a 'cliffhanger' of sorts- what will the disciples now do?

General Information about the book of MARK:

Mark describes Jesus as being both a divine King and a compassionate human- truly God and truly man. Mark's gospel is divided into three parts:
- The first part introduces Jesus as the Son of God, the new King of the Jews
- The second part shows Jesus' disciples attempting to understand who Jesus is
- The third part shows Jesus as the Savior

Content Highlights:
- John the Baptist prepares the way
- The baptism of Jesus, Jesus' temptation in the desert.
- Jesus' earthly ministry – calls and instructs His disciples, parables, miracles, teachings
- John the Baptist beheaded
- The transfiguration
- Jesus predicts his death three times
- Jesus' final week- the Triumphal Entry, cleansing the Temple, the Lord's Supper
- Additional teachings, signs of the end of the age, the great tribulation
- Jesus' arrest, crucifixion, burial, and resurrection
- The Great Commission

Note:
- Jesus is Lord of the Sabbath (chapter 2:23-3:6)
- The Unforgivable Sin (chapter 3:28-30)
- Mark reports Jesus' miracles in greater detail than the other gospels.
- Mark uses Roman days, which begin at midnight, not Jewish days which began at sunset.

For even the Son of Man did not come to be served, but to serve, and to give His life as a ransom for many.
Mark 10:45 NIV

KEY Verses
- 2:17
- 2:27-28
- 7:14-23
- 8:34-36
- 10:13-16
- 12:29-31
- 13:24-27

Theme: Jesus Christ as a suffering servant.

LUKE

Literary Style: Gospel, Historical Narrative, Poetry

New Testament Book #: 3
# of chapters: 24

Author: Luke, a physician and traveling companion of Paul. Luke wrote this gospel in either Rome or Caesarea.

Audience: Specifically addressed to Theophilus, a Greek or Roman dignitary, but it contains information helpful for Christians of all nations throughout history.

Setting: Bethlehem, Nazareth, Galilee and Judea. Events recorded in Luke took place from about 5 BC to AD 33, during Jesus' lifetime.

Of Interest: Probably written AD 62-63, around the same time as Acts. (Before the fall of Jerusalem in AD 70). It is the first book in a two-volume set, known as Luke-Acts.

General Information about the book of LUKE:
- Luke specifically states that he wrote this book to record an orderly account of Jesus' ministry. He has carefully researched the details and includes proper titles, names, and locations of people and events.
- Luke is considered the church's first historian.
- As a physician, Luke pays special attention to medical terminology and diseases. He also mentions the poor and women more than any other gospel.
- Luke includes the most detailed account of Jesus' birth.

Content Highlights:
- The angel Gabriel predicts the birth of both John the Baptist and Jesus, the promised Messiah.
- The birth of Jesus Christ, presentation at the Temple, flight into Egypt
- Jesus in the Temple at age twelve
- The baptism of Jesus, the temptation of Jesus in the wilderness
- Genealogy of Jesus from Joseph to Adam
- Jesus' earthly ministry – He calls and instructs His disciples, parables, miracles, teachings
- The transfiguration
- Signs of the end of the age
- Jesus' final week, the Lord's Supper
- Jesus' arrest, crucifixion, burial, and resurrection
- The Great Commission to the Disciples, and the Ascension of Jesus

Note:
- Mary's Song-The Magnificat (chapter 1:46-55)
- The Beatitudes (chapter 6:20-23)
- The Lord's Prayer (chapter 11:2-4)
- Zacchaeus the tax collector (chapter 19:1-10)
- The Road to Emmaus (chapter 24:35)

For where your treasure is, there your heart will be also.
Luke 12:34 NIV

KEY Verses:
- 1:26-36
- 2:10-14
- 3:7-9
- 5:31-32
- 6:27-36
- 6:41-42
- 8:21
- 10:25-28
- 11:9-13
- 12:8-10
- 12:34
- 21:25-28
- 24:44-53

Theme: Jesus Christ is Savior for all who believe in Him.

JOHN

Literary Style: Gospel, Historical Narrative, Poetry

New Testament Book #: 4
# of chapters: 21

Author > Attributed to John, a Galilean fisherman called to be a disciple and member of Jesus' inner circle. Brother of the apostle James, these sons of Zebedee were called *Boanerges* (Sons of Thunder) by Jesus.

Audience > Written to unbelievers- mostly to Greek speaking Jews living outside of Israel. John explains Jewish customs and translates Aramaic words into Greek.

Setting > Galilee and Judea. Events which occurred during Jesus' earthly ministry, around AD 30-33.

Of Interest > Polycarp, an acquaintance of John's reported John wrote this book while serving the church in Ephesus. Likely written near the end of John's life, while in exile on the island of Patmos AD 85-95.

General Information about the book of JOHN:

- The word, *logos* in Greek is translated as *reason*, or *principle*. By using the word *logos* in his first chapter, John introduces Jesus as the reason behind the universe. He was present at creation and is one with God.
- John includes seven I AM statements which show who Jesus is. These statements include- I AM... the bread of life (6:35, 41), the light of the world (8:12, 9:5), the gate for the sheep (10:7, 9), the good shepherd (10:11, 14), the resurrection and the life (11:25), the way the truth and the life (14:6). the true vine (15:1,5).
- John includes seven signs (wonders) in his gospel. These signs provide evidence of Christ's deity.

Content Highlights:

- Prologue, which introduces Jesus as the Word (Logos) become flesh, to dwell among men
- John the Baptist's ministry
- Jesus' ministry- teachings, parables, and the seven signs, which are:
    1. Turns water into wine
    2. Heals an official's son
    3. Heals the sick
    4. Feeds the five thousand
    5. Walks on water
    6. Heals a blind man
    7. Raises Lazarus from the dead
- Jesus' final week, the Last Supper, betrayal, trial, death and resurrection
- Jesus' appearance to his disciples after his resurrection
- Epilogue, which indicates Jesus did many more signs and wonders that were not written down

Note:
- John calls himself 'the one whom Jesus loved'
- Has about 90% unique material not found in the other three gospels (Matthew, Mark, Luke).
- Early manuscripts do not include chapter 7:53-8:11, the story of the adulteress woman whom Jesus forgave.

For God so loved the world that he gave his one and only Son, that whoever believes in him shall not perish but have eternal life.
John 3:16 NIV

KEY Verses
- 1:1-5, 12
- 3:5, 16-17
- 4:24
- 5:24
- 8:12, 32
- 10:30
- 11:25
- 13:34
- 14:1, 6, 15
- 15:5

Theme > Jesus Christ is the divine Son of God- who was, who is, and who is to come.

ACTS OF THE APOSTLES

Literary Style: Historical Narrative

New Testament Book #: 5
# of chapters: 28

Author › Attributed to Luke, a traveling companion of the apostle Paul. Educated as a physician, evidence suggests he was a Gentile who knew the Hebrew scriptures.

Audience › Written to a specific person, Theophilus who was likely a high-ranking Roman citizen. The message of Acts is intended for Christians throughout history.

Setting › Probably written AD 60-62, Acts documents events which occurred after Jesus' ascension-Pentecost, the early church in Jerusalem, Antioch, and the spread of the gospel to Greece, Asia Minor.

Of Interest › Known officially as Acts of the Apostles, it is a record of early Christian church history.

General Information about the book of ACTS:
- Jesus had asked his disciples to remain in Jerusalem and wait for the helper He promised to them. They prayerfully chose an apostle to replace Judas, a man named Mathias who had witnessed Jesus' ministry.
- Pentecost was the outpouring of the promised Holy Spirit to the believers gathered in Jerusalem.
- Peter spoke to the crowds gathered and 3,000 believers were added that day (ch. 2:41).
- The apostles showed love- they healed the sick, cast out demons in Jesus name, and boldly proclaimed the gospel message – hope and salvation through repentance and belief in Jesus Christ, evidenced by new life.

Content Highlights:
- The ascension of Jesus into heaven, witnessed by the apostles
- Matthias is chosen to replace Judas as the twelfth apostle.
- Pentecost, the beginning of the Christian church.
- Apostles preach, teach, heal, and cast our demons in Jerusalem and surrounding areas. Thousands believe.
- The unbelief of the Jewish leaders, the arrest of the apostles, the first Christian martyr, Stephen.
- The conversion of Saul to Paul (ch. 9 and ch. 26).
- Paul and Barnabas are sent by the church in Antioch on their first missionary journey to Asia Minor (ch. 13-14).
- Paul and Timothy spread the gospel in Greece and Asia Minor (ch. 16-18a).
- Paul's third missionary journey, he travels in Asia Minor and Greece. He is arrested and imprisoned, later sent via ship to Rome for his trial. He is shipwrecked on Malta, preaches there, then finally arrives in Rome.

Note ›
- The Jerusalem Council held in AD 49/50 (ch. 15) ended the dispute between Jews and Gentiles on several topics including circumcision, unclean food.. It was decided that Gentiles did not have to obey the Mosaic laws.
- The early church was called The Way (ch. 19:23).

Peter replied, "Repent and be baptized, every one of you, in the name of Jesus Christ for the forgiveness of your sins. And you will receive the gift of the Holy Spirit."
Acts 2:38 NIV

KEY Verses ›
- 1:8,11
- 2:17
- 2:21, 36-38
- 3:19
- 4:11-12, 32
- 17:22-28
- 20:28
- 20:35
- 26:15-18
- 28:3-6

Theme › Jesus Christ is the Savior, the hope and salvation of the world, for both Jews and Gentiles.

ROMANS

Literary Style: Epistle (letter)

New Testament Book #: 6
# of chapters: 16

Author: Paul wrote this letter in AD 57 from the city of Corinth, during his third missionary journey.

Audience: Written to the church in Rome, which was a mix of both Jewish and Gentile believers.

Setting: Roman emperor Claudius had evicted Jews from the city of Rome in AD 49, leaving the Gentile believers to establish house churches. When Claudius died, the Jewish refugees returned to Rome.

Of Interest: Nero was the current Roman Emperor, but it was a time of relative peace. The great fire of Rome – which Nero blamed on the Christians, had not yet occurred.

General Information about the book of ROMANS:
- Romans was written to give clarity to the church- to remind them
    1. all are guilty of sin and deserve death
    2. believers are saved by God's grace through faith alone- not works
    3. the renewing work of the Holy Spirit within believers
- Paul uses the body as an image of the church. Just as the body has many parts, so the church has many believers which each contribute their individual gifts to benefit the church as a whole.
- The purpose of the Torah's 613 laws as a reminder of the sinfulness of the human heart, of man's inability to keep them all perfectly.

Content Highlights:
- Part One (Chapters 1-4): All man are sinful, unable to keep the laws of Moses. Man needs a Savior.
- Part Two (Chapters 5-8): Jesus is the Savior who freely offers salvation to those who believe in Him.
- Part Three (Chapters 9-11): Explanation of the covenants- God chose a specific family to be His people, when they rejected Jesus as the Messiah, the covenantal promises were expanded to include Gentiles.
- Part Four (Chapters 12-16): Unity in the church- respect each other's differences, love and serve one another, the importance of forgiveness and reconciliation among believers.

Note:
- Paul (also known as Saul) had been a Pharisee - a strict observer of the Mosaic laws. He had an encounter with God while traveling to Damascus which changed the trajectory of his life- from persecutor to evangelist.
- Romans is the longest epistle in the New Testament.
- Justification- to be counted as righteous (holy) before God due to Christ's atonement for our sins.

For all have sinned and fall short of the glory of God and are justified freely by His grace through the redemption that came by Christ Jesus.
Romans 3:23-24 NIV

KEY Verses:
- 1:16
- 2:6-7
- 3:9-20
- 3:23-24
- 5:8
- 5:18-21
- 6:1-2, 7
- 6:4
- 6:23
- 8:28
- 8:38-39
- 10:9
- 12:1-2
- 12:19-21

Theme: The Holy Spirit works within believers to produce lives of righteousness and justification.

1 CORINTHIANS

Literary Style: Epistle (letter)

New Testament Book #: 7
# of chapters: 16

Author: Paul wrote this letter in AD 55 while visiting Ephesus during his third missionary journey. Written in a literary style, Paul uses irony, repetition and alliteration to emphasize his points.

Audience: Written to the church in Corinth, a mix of Jewish and Gentile believers.

Setting: Paul had spent about 18 months with the church in Corinth, so was familiar with many of its members. Corinth was known for its pagan temples, and their associated sexual immorality.

Of Interest: References to another letter (5:9) suggests that this is Paul's second letter to the church in Corinth. His first letter (the "sorrowful letter") did not survive and is not included in the biblical canon.

General Information about the book of FIRST CORINTHIANS:

- Paul wrote this letter to the church in Corinth to offer advice and explain doctrine, to address and correct wrong practices among the believers, and to encourage them in their faith.

Content Highlights:

- Chapters 1-4 deals with divisions in the church.
- Chapters 5-7 addresses sexual sin, specifically temple prostitutes and incest.
- Chapters 8-10 clarifies issues the Jews and Gentiles are having with traditional Jewish food laws.
- Chapters 11-14 emphasizes the role of the church- to be unified, have orderly services, accountable to one another, and to avoid quarrels and division.
- Chapter 13 a poem about love.
- Chapters 15 tackles questions the church was having with the resurrection of the dead.
- Chapter 16 Paul asks the church to set aside money for the church in Jerusalem. He writes of his travel plans, and that they are to welcome Timothy when he visits.

Note: Paul was planning to visit the church in Corinth, but when he heard reports of confusion about the resurrection, division, rivalry, and sexual sin among the church members he decided these issues needed to be addressed immediately, they could not wait.

> *Do you not know that your bodies are temples of the Holy Spirit, who is in you, whom you have received from God? ...Therefore honor God with your bodies.*
> 1 Corinthians 6:19,20 NIV

KEY Verses:
- 1:18
- 3:16-17
- 6:9-11
- 9:6
- 10:31
- 13:4-7
- 15:58
- 16:13

Theme: Christians are to be lights in this dark world, to live out their faith among unbelievers.

2 CORINTHIANS

Literary Style: Composite Epistle (letters)

New Testament Book #: 8 | # of chapters: 13

Author: Paul wrote this letter in AD 56 during his third missionary journey. It is believed he wrote this during his stay in Philippi.

Audience: Written to the church in Corinth, a mix of Jewish and Gentile believers. Corinth was known for its pagan temples, and their associated sexual immorality.

Setting: Paul had a brief stay in Corinth after Timothy delivered his second letter, which we call 1 Corinthians. According to Timothy, despite Pauls' letter the church continued to deal with division and quarrels.

Of Interest: Scholars believe that this book is a composite letter, containing two or more letters from Paul to the church at Corinth. Inconsistencies in tone between chapters 9 and 10 suggest this.

General Information about the book of SECOND CORINTHIANS:
- After receiving Timothy's poor report on the status of the church in Corinth, Paul sent Titus to visit them.
- Titus' report was positive, and Paul wrote this letter in response to these promising reports. He forgives the church in Corinth and wishes to reconcile, to restore his relationship with them.
- Aware some believers have not yet repented; Paul encourages them to submit to the church's authority.

Content Highlights:
- Paul warns the church to live transformed lives, to value what Jesus valued- humility, weakness, generosity, and to show love and concern for others.
- Paul expresses relief and joy at the church's restoration and unity.
- Paul encourages the Corinthian church to give generously, specifically to the church in Jerusalem (which had experienced a famine in AD 44-48).
- Paul discovers the Corinthian church prefers other leaders over him, that they are embarrassed by Paul's poverty, unrefined speech. He defends himself as an apostle chosen by Christ, and responsible for establishing their church. He compares his life to that of Christs- poor, humble and suffering, and rejected.

Therefore, if anyone is in Christ, he is a new creation; the old has gone, the new has come!
2 Corinthians 5:17 NIV

Note:
- Acts chapter 18 tells the story of how the Corinthian church began.
- This book provides some personal information about the apostle Paul, it mentions the 'thorn in his flesh'.

KEY Verses:
- 3:4-6
- 3:17-18
- 4:3-4
- 4:17-18
- 5:9-10
- 5:20-21
- 6:14
- 9:6-8, 15
- 13:5

Theme: Believers in Christ must live transformed lives and avoid the deception of Satan.

GALATIANS

Literary Style: Epistle (letter)

New Testament Book # **9**   # of chapters **6**

Author — Paul wrote this letter either shortly before or shortly after attending the Jerusalem Council, which occurred in AD 49 or 50.

Audience — Written to the churches located in the Roman province of Galatia, in Asia Minor, now Turkey. The Galatian churches included those in Antioch, Lystra, Derbe, and Iconium.

Setting — Paul had been traveling for 18 months on his first missionary journey and was now in Antioch, the city where the first church was planted.

Of Interest — Paul and Barnabas were called to Jerusalem to report on their teachings to the Gentile churches, as they radically differed from what the church leaders in Jerusalem were teaching.

General Information about the book of GALATIANS:
- Paul begins with a warning to the churches to remain true to the gospel of Christ, not to be deceived by false teachings, specifically regarding justification by faith. This was contrary to what the Jerusalem churches were teaching- that converts must submit to the Mosaic law, become circumcised in order to be accepted into the church family.
- Paul defends his apostolic authority in the first two chapters.
- The book of Galatians includes details of Paul's life not included in the book of Acts- his time in Arabia (1:17-18), his visit with Peter, his confrontation of Peter (2:11-21), and the Jerusalem Council (2:1-10).

Content Highlights:
- Paul provides his credentials as an apostle of Christ, chosen by God.
- Paul writes about the Abrahamic covenant- its promise, and the purpose of the Mosaic law with its limitations.
- Paul writes about the freedom which the new covenant in Christ provides. The freedom from rituals and laws (legalism) which had a temporary purpose until Christ the Messiah fulfilled the law. The new covenant includes all who believe in Christ as their Savior, both Jews and Gentiles. Acceptance into this new covenant is by faith alone, not by deeds – it cannot be earned but is a gift from God.
- The Fruit of the Spirit, (chapter 5:22) is evidence of a life led by the Holy Spirit. A new life transformed into the image of Christ.

Note
- At the time of the Council of Jerusalem "The Way of Christianity' was considered a Jewish sect.
- The decision of the council was that James, John, and Peter would concentrate on Jewish believers, while Paul and Barnabas would evangelize among the Gentiles.

> I have been crucified with Christ and I no longer live, but Christ lives in me. The life I now live in the body, I live by faith in the Son of God, who loved me and gave himself for me.
> Galatians 2:20 NIV

KEY Verses
- 2:3
- 2:15-21
- 3:13-14
- 3:27-29
- 4:4-7
- 5:1-4
- 5:14, 22
- 6:7-8

Theme — Salvation by grace, not works.

EPHESIANS

Literary Style: Prison Epistle (letter)

New Testament Book #: 10
# of chapters: 6

Author: Paul wrote this letter in AD 60-61 while in prison (either in Rome or Caesarea, most scholars believe he was in Rome).

Audience: Written to the church in Ephesus.

Setting: Paul wrote this letter around the same time he wrote Colossians and Philemon, and all three books were given to Tychicus to deliver.

Of Interest: Ephesians is known as one of the four "prison epistles". Details of Paul's time in Ephesus can be found in Acts chapter 19.

General Information about the book of EPHESIANS:
- This is one of Paul's most formal letters.
- Ephesians shares similar ideas with the book of Colossians.

Content Highlights:
- Begins with a poem praising God for all He has done.
- Chapters 1-3 contain the gospel message of salvation:
  - - the mercy and grace of God
  - acceptance and unity as members of Gods family, through Christ's atonement for our sins
  - Christ lives within those who believe in Him as their Savior
- Chapter 4-6 Paul writes about how the believer lives their life. He addresses:
  - unity among believers, though each has their own place and purpose in the family of God.
  - how family members are to relate and treat one another.
  - Practical advice on living renewed lives- be truthful, kind, honest, control your tongue, etc.
  - Be prepared to defend against evil, warnings about spiritual warfare.

Note: Believers must put on the full armor of God, to stand firm against the devil's schemes. This includes:
- the belt of truth buckled around your waist
- the breastplate of righteousness
- have feet fitted with the readiness that comes from the gospel of peace
- the shield of faith
- the helmet of salvation
- the sword of the Spirit, which is the word of God.

"Therefore be imitators of God, as beloved children. And walk in love, as Christ loved us and gave Himself up for us, a fragrant offering and sacrifice to God."
Ephesians 5:1-2 NIV

KEY Verses:
- 1:7
- 2:4-5
- 2:8-9
- 2:18-20
- 3:6
- 4:15
- 5:33
- 6:4

Theme: What it means to be a Christian- believers die to their old selves; and live new lives in submission to Jesus Christ.

PHILIPPIANS

Literary Style: Prison Epistle (letter)

New Testament Book #: 11
# of chapters: 4

Author: Paul wrote this letter in AD 61-62, near the end of his first imprisonment in Rome.

Audience: Written to the church in Philippi. Paul had a relationship with them, he spent about 3 months with this church during his second missionary journey.

Setting: Philippi was a Roman colony in Macedonia, many soldiers lived in this city. Epaphroditus had brought a gift from the Philippian church to Paul and was sent home with this letter.

Of Interest: Church members included Lydia, and the jailer who witnessed the earthquake free Paul from prison.

General Information about the book of PHILIPPIANS:
- This is Paul's most affectionately personal letter. It was written to express gratitude for the church's gift, rather than in response to a crisis within the church.
- Paul tells the story of his conversion.

Content Highlights:
- Paul divides this letter into two parts:
    1. Theological truths.
        - Salvation
    2. Christian living.
        - Unity in the church
        - Avoid legalism
        - Stewardship
        - Imitate Christ
        - Be content in all circumstances

Do nothing out of selfish ambition or vain conceit, but in humility consider others as more important than yourselves.
Philippians 2:3 NIV

- Philippians 2:6-11 is a poem containing the gospel message. **Note**
- Paul shares personal information in chapter 3, he is a circumcised Jew of the tribe of Benjamin and was a law-abiding Pharisee.

KEY Verses
- 1:9-11
- 1:20-24
- 2:3-4
- 2:12-13
- 3:18-21
- 4:8-9
- 4:13
- 4:19

Theme: To encourage the church in spiritual growth, their commitment to God and to one another.

COLOSSIANS

Literary Style: Prison Epistle (letter)

New Testament Book # 12 | # of chapters 4

Author: Paul wrote this letter in AD 60-61 while in prison (either in Rome or Caesarea, most scholars believe he was in Rome).

Audience: Written to the church in Colossae, a mix of Jews and Gentiles. Epaphras had established this church, Paul had not yet visited them, so he did not have a personal relationship with the church.

Setting: Paul wrote this letter around the same time he wrote Ephesians and Philemon, and all three books were given to Tychicus to deliver.

Of Interest: One of the four prison epistles.
Colossae, known for its fine wool (called Colossinum), was located on a trade route to the Orient.

General Information about the book of COLOSSIANS:
- The church in Colossae had a mix of Jewish and Gentile believers and was influenced by Greek culture and Jewish traditions, including polytheism and observance of the Torah laws.
- Paul wrote this to challenge a heretical teaching which claimed Jesus was not really God (possibly a result of combining the beliefs of Judaism and an early form of Gnosticism).
- Paul teaches Christ is the visible image of the sovereign God, who has authority from God, and is the head of the church.
- Paul challenges the Colossian church to a greater devotion to Jesus. He reminds them what becoming Christ-like is - a complete transformation in thought, word and deed.

Content Highlights:
- Introduction – greeting, a prayer for spiritual growth of the church
- The nature of Christ, who He is
- What Christ did for us
- The believer's new life in Christ

Note:
- Paul was imprisoned with a fellow Christian named Aristarchus (4:10).
- Colossians is closely related to the books of Ephesians and Philemon, sharing similar outlines and ideas. These three books were written while Paul was in prison.

So then, just as you received Christ Jesus as Lord, continue to live your lives in him, rooted and built up in him, strengthened in the faith as you were taught, and overflowing with thankfulness.
Colossians 2:6-7 NIV

KEY Verses:
- 1:13-14
- 1:15-20
- 1:21-22
- 2:6-7
- 2:9-10
- 2:20-23
- 3:2
- 3:12-13
- 3:15
- 3:17
- 3:23-24
- 4:2

Theme: Believers are to die to their sinful life and live new, transformed lives in submission to Jesus Christ.

1 THESSALONIANS

Literary Style: Epistle (letter)

New Testament Book # 13 | # of chapters 5

Author: Paul wrote this letter while in Corinth around AD 50-51, shortly after planting the church in Thessalonica during his second missionary journey.

Audience: Written to the church in Thessalonica, a mix of Jewish and Gentile (mostly Greek) believers. The church was being persecuted for refusing to worship Roman Emperor Caesar.

Setting: Thessalonica was the capitol of the Roman province of Macedonia. A large port city, it was known for Emperor worship, and the Cabiri cult.

Of Interest: Paul was forced to leave Thessalonica, as he had been accused of treason. Known today as Thessaloniki, it is one of the few remaining cities from the New Testament era.

General Information about the book of FIRST THESSALONIANS:
- Paul was forced to leave Thessalonica in a hurry, he went to Athens with Timothy and Silas (also known as Silvanus). He sent Timothy back to check on the church and received a mostly good report- they were growing despite persecution but had a misunderstanding about the return of Christ.
- Paul wrote this letter to encourage, reassure, and correct misunderstandings. It seems several members of this church had died, and the believers were concerned that the dead would miss out on Christ's return.

Content Highlights:

Chapters 1-3
- Paul begins his letter with a greeting, expressing thanksgiving for the church's holding steadfast to the faith despite opposition. He expresses a desire to visit, and reports on Timothy's visit.
- He prays for the church to continue to grow and remain in Christ, to live in holiness.

Chapter 4
- Paul gives instructions on holy living.
- He assures them regarding their misunderstanding of death- that those who are believers will go to heaven when Christ returns.

Chapter 5
- Paul encourages them to be ready for the day of the Lord.
- He ends the book with specific reminders of holy living, and a blessing.

Note:
- Chapter 4:16-18 refers to Jesus' second coming. Paul uses the word *arpadzw*, or 'snatched away'. Jerome translates this word as *rapere* – or rapture in English. This passage has sparked debate among believers as to a pre, mid, or postmillennial tribulation removal of the church from earth.
- In fact, Paul does not include a timeframe for Christ's return, but assures the church that no one will be left behind.

Be joyful always; pray continually; give thanks in all circumstances, for this is God's will for you in Christ Jesus.
1 Thessalonians 5:16-18 NIV

KEY Verses:
- 2:3-4
- 3:2-4
- 3:11-13
- 4:3-8
- 4:13-18
- 5:1-11
- 5:14-22

Theme: Remain faithful in all circumstances.

2 THESSALONIANS

Literary Style: Epistle (letter)

New Testament Book # 14   # of chapters 3

Author: Paul wrote this letter while in Corinth with Timothy and Silas (Timotheus and Silvanus).

Audience: Written to the church in Thessalonica, located in Macedonia (northern Greece).

Setting: It is believed that Paul wrote this letter in AD 50-51, shortly after he wrote his first letter to Thessalonica, and 3-4 years before Paul visited them for a second time.

Of Interest: In chapter 3:17 Paul asks the church to note his handwriting, lest they be deceived by counterfeit letters.

General Information about the book of SECOND THESSALONIANS:
- This letter has a similar theme as Paul's first letter to this church:
  - encouragement
  - stand firm against false teachers
  - hope despite persecution

Content Highlights:
- Chapter 1: Hope despite persecution.
  - God is in control; He will avenge those who persecute His people.
  - Paul encourages them to endure these earthly trials patiently as the faithful will be rewarded.
- Chapter 2: The Day of the Lord.
  - Describes events which must take place before Christ returns.
  - Warns against deception, false signs and wonders.
  - God's people are chosen for salvation, stand firm in the faith and be encouraged.
- Chapter 3: Christian Living
  - Believers must work to support themselves and to benefit others.

Note:
- This book is the only one which mentions the 'man of lawlessness'.
- Some scholars believe this book was dictated by Paul and transcribed by perhaps Timothy or Silas (see Paul's greeting in 3:17).

> *But the Lord is faithful, and He will strengthen and protect you from the evil one.*
> 2 Thessalonians 3:3 NIV

KEY Verses:
- 1:2
- 1:10-12
- 2:3
- 2:10-12
- 3:5
- 3:13

Theme: Stand firm in the faith, be encouraged, have hope for the future.

1 TIMOTHY

Literary Style: Pastoral Epistle (letter)

New Testament Book # 15 | # of chapters 6

Author: Paul wrote this letter around AD 62-63.

Audience: Written to Timothy, a young pastor and fellow missionary whom Paul had met about 10 years prior. After mentoring him, Paul sent Timothy to minister to the churches in Ephesus, Corinth, and Philippi.

Setting: Paul was in Macedonia, and Timothy was pastoring the church in Ephesus. This letter was written just prior to Roman Emperor Nero's persecution of the Christians began in AD 63.

Of Interest: Timothy's mother (Eunice) and grandmother (Lois) were faithful believers living in Lystra. Timothy's father was a Greek (Acts 16:1). Paul was a mentor and father figure to Timothy (1:2).

General Information about the book of FIRST TIMOTHY:

- Paul writes this letter to Timothy to provide guidance for orderly worship and proper church leadership

Content Highlights:
- Chapter 1
    - Warnings against false doctrine.
    - The Testimony of Paul.
- Chapter 2
    - Instructions on prayer, worship, submission of women in the church.
- Chapter 3-4
    - Conduct and behavior, moral character of overseers (elders and deacons) of the church.
    - Relationships within families and households.
- Chapter 5
    - Ministry to widows
    - Church discipline
- Chapter 6
    - Warnings against false doctrine.
    - Encouragement to persevere, to "fight the good fight" (6:12).
    - Instructs the rich to be generous, share their wealth.

- Recently the authorship of this letter has been questioned, citing differences in vocabulary and style. Paul may have used a scribe to compose this letter, or it may be a later work compiled from Pauls' teachings. **Note**

> *For there is one God and one mediator between God and men, the man Christ Jesus.*
> 1 Timothy 2:5 NIV

KEY Verses
- 1:5
- 1:8
- 1:16
- 2:1-4
- 2:5-6
- 2:12
- 3:2-13
- 4:4
- 6:7-10
- 6:18-19

Theme: Instructions for church structure and leadership, the behavior of church members.

2 TIMOTHY

Literary Style: Pastoral Epistle (letter)

New Testament Book #: 16
# of chapters: 4

Author: Paul wrote this letter from prison in Rome around AD 67, just prior to his death.

Audience: Written to Timothy, a young pastor and fellow missionary whom Paul had met about 10 years prior. After mentoring him, Paul sent Timothy to minister to the churches in Ephesus, Corinth, and Philippi.

Setting: Paul was in a Roman prison, and Timothy was pastoring the church in Ephesus. Paul longs to see Timothy again and asks him to visit soon, and to bring Mark, as he has been abandoned by all but Luke.

Of Interest: Paul was a mentor and father figure to Timothy (1:2). This letter has a more personal tone than 1 Timothy.

General Information about the book of SECOND TIMOTHY:
- Paul writes this letter to Timothy to remind him that being a believer is not without risk, suffering, or challenges. He encourages Timothy to remain strong in the faith and to remember that in times of darkness Christ's loving care is most tangible.
- Paul encourages Timothy to be bold, to use his spiritual gifts to spread the gospel.
- Paul uses the words 'be bold' several times in both 1 and 2 Timothy.

Content Highlights:
- Chapter 1
  - Paul encourages Timothy to be bold, unashamed of the gospel, and to remain true to sound doctrine.
- Chapter 2
  - Assurance of salvation
  - Urges Timothy to live out his faith, avoid quarrels, show love, pursue righteousness and peace.
- Chapter 3
  - Warnings of difficulties ahead, temptations, and struggles believers will face.
- Chapter 4
  - Paul urges Timothy to preach the word to all and in all circumstances.
  - Remain true to sound doctrine, do not preach what people want to hear, preach the truth.
  - A request for Timothy to visit soon, to bring Mark, Paul's coat and his scrolls.

Note:
- Paul writes with the urgency of one who knows their time on earth is coming to an end.
- Tradition says the apostles Peter and Paul were executed under Nero's order. in AD 67 or 68. Peter was crucified, Paul (a Roman citizen) was beheaded. Nero died in AD 68.

> *All Scripture is God-breathed and is useful for teaching, rebuking, correcting and training in righteousness, so that the servant of God may be thoroughly equipped for every good work.*
> 2 Timothy 3:16-17 NIV

KEY Verses:
- 1:9
- 1:12
- 2:10-13
- 2:19
- 2:22-26
- 3:1-5
- 3:16-17
- 4:2-4
- 4:7
- 4:18

Theme: Proclaim the truth of the gospel without shame or fear.

TITUS

Literary Style: Pastoral Epistle (letter)

New Testament Book #: 17
# of chapters: 3

Author: Written by Paul around AD 63, following his release from prison in Rome. Paul probably wrote this while traveling from Ephesus or Corinth to Nicopolis, where he asks Titus to join him for the winter.

Audience: This is a personal letter written to Titus, Paul's co-worker and leader of the churches on Crete. Titus was a Greek speaking Gentile believer who had accompanied Paul to the Council of Jerusalem.

Setting: Crete, a Greek island and Roman province was infamous as a violent, unsafe, and morally corrupt area. Its capital city, Gortyn had temples dedicated to Apollo and the Egyptian gods.

Of Interest: Crete had a sizable Jewish population, and several Cretan Jews were present at Pentecost.

General Information about the book of Titus:
- This letter is very similar to Paul's first letter to Timothy- the subject matter and phrases used.

Content Highlights:
- Chapter 1
  - Paul instructs Titus to appoint elders to oversee the churches.
  - Provides guidance for selecting these elders.
  - A warning/admonition to remove those who preach false doctrine from roles of authority.
- Chapter 2
  - Instruction on Christian behavior.
  - Preach sound doctrine.
  - Reassurance of salvation.
- Chapter 3
  - The state of man before salvation.
  - Proper conduct towards others.
  - God's grace and love motivates believers to live renewed lives through the presence of the Holy Spirit.
  - A request for Timothy to assist fellow leaders, and to visit Paul in Nicopolis.

> In everything set them an example by doing what is good. In your teaching show integrity, seriousness and soundness of speech that cannot be condemned,
> Titus 2:7-8 NIV

Note:
- Paul accompanied Titus to Crete and together they preached the gospel in that area.
- Titus was placed in charge of the church community on the island around AD 57.

KEY Verses:
- 1:1-2
- 1:15-16
- 2:1
- 2:6-8
- 2:11-15
- 3:1-3
- 3:6-7

Theme: Believers are to model their lives after Jesus Christ, who is our God and Savior.

PHILEMON

Literary Style: Prison Epistle (letter)

New Testament Book # **18** | # of chapters **1**

Author: Written by Paul around AD 60-62, while in prison in Rome. Paul had completed his three missionary journeys. This letter was written around the same time as Ephesians, Philippians and Colossians.

Audience: This is a personal letter written to Philemon, a wealthy man who led a house-church in Colossae. The church met in Philemon's home (vs. 2).

Setting: Philemon had slaves, and one of them (Onesimus) had robbed Philemon and ran away. Paul ministered to Onesimus, (while in the Roman prison- vs. 10) and Onesimus became a Christian.

Of Interest: According to Roman law Paul was required to return Onesimus to his master.

General Information about the book of PHILEMON:

- Paul was with Timothy when he wrote this letter.
- Paul is familiar with the congregation and greets church members by name.
- Paul prays for fellow believers, that their work may be effective.

Content Highlights:

- This letter addresses a specific believer, Philemon urging him to accept his slave Onesimus as an equal, despite his status and unlawful behavior.
- Paul asks that grace, forgiveness, and love to be shown to Onesimus who has become a brother in Christ.
- Paul sees that good has come from a seemingly bad situation.
- Paul seeks to obey the law, though he wishes to have Onesimus remain in Rome and assist him while he is imprisoned. He offers to repay Philemon for any debt Onesimus owes, and trusts Philemon to act fairly.

> *I pray that your partnership with us in the faith may be effective in deepening your understanding of every good thing we share for the sake of Christ.*
> Philemon 1:6 NIV

Note:
- Philemon is the shortest and most personal of Paul's letters.
- Onesimus in Greek means *useful*.
- This is the only letter where Paul doesn't mention Jesus' death or resurrection.

KEY Verses:
- 1:3
- 1:4-6
- 1:15-16
- 1:25

Theme: Forgiveness and acceptance of one another as brothers and sisters in Christ.

HEBREWS

Literary Style: Epistle, Homily, Sermon

New Testament Book #: 19
# of chapters: 13

Author: Not identified. Many authors have been proposed- Silas, Luke, Clement, Barnabas, Timothy, Apollos, Philip, Peter, Jude and Aristian. What we do know is the author had not heard Jesus preach (2:3).

Audience: Probably Jewish Christians, which is where the book gets its name. Hebrews includes the history of the Israelites and Old Testament scripture.

Setting: Written before the fall of Jerusalem in AD 70, as destruction of the Temple is not mentioned. Likely written during Nero's persecution of Christians in Rome, AD 64-68.

Of Interest: Jews were exempt from Emperor worship, but Christians were persecuted if they didn't participate. Some Jewish Christians considered returning to Judaism, to avoid persecution.

General Information about the book of HEBREWS:
- Believers were facing persecution, and some were abandoning the faith.
- The author of Hebrews seeks to depict Jesus as God- far superior to the Old Testament prophets and leaders.

Content Highlights:
- Chapters 1-4 The Supremacy of Christ
  - Compares Jesus to the angels.
  - Compares Jesus to Moses and Joshua.
  - A call to hear and believe in Christ as Savior, our deliverer sent from God.
- Chapters 4-7 Jesus as our perfect high priest.
  - He provides our Sabbath rest.
- Chapters 8-10 The Old and New Covenants
- Chapter 10 Jesus as the perfect sacrifice- who died once, for all.
  - Live Godly lives, refrain from sin.
- Chapter 11 Faithful living, gives examples from the Old Testament.
  - If they remain faithful to Christ, God will not abandon them.
- Chapters 12-13 Remain faithful, serve God and anticipate Christ's return.

Note:
- The author wants to convince readers to remain true to Christianity, do not turn back to the Jewish beliefs and traditions. He includes many Old testament references to argue his point.
- The author encourages believers to grow in their faith.

So Christ was sacrificed once to take away the sins of many; and he will appear a second time, not to bear sin, but to bring salvation to those who are waiting for him.
Hebrews 9:28 NIV

KEY Verses:
- 1:1-4
- 2:2, 14-18
- 3:1, 6
- 4:12-13
- 5:9
- 6:13-20
- 7:26-27
- 8:10-13
- 9:25-28
- 10:4
- 10:10-16
- 10:24-25
- 10:30
- 11:1
- 11:6
- 12:7-13
- 12:14
- 13:2, 5, 8
- 13:17

Theme: Jesus is the Messiah who fulfilled the law and the Old Testament prophecies.

JAMES

Literary Style: Universal/General Epistle (letter)

New Testament Book #: 20
# of chapters: 5

Author: James, the brother of Jesus. He was not a follower while Jesus was alive, but accepted Christ as the Messiah when Jesus appeared to him after His resurrection.

Audience: This letter is addressed to the "twelve tribes dispersed abroad"- Jewish Christians outside of Palestine.

Setting: Probably written between AD 45-48, prior to the Jerusalem Council.

Of Interest: He was known as 'James the Righteous' (aka 'Just') and was leader of the church in Jerusalem.

General Information about the book of JAMES:

- This book challenges Christians to live righteous lives, to show the world 'faith in action'.
- James is considered the first New Testament book to have been written (no mention of Gentile Christians).

Content Highlights:

- Contains twelve short teachings on faith and behavior, including:
    - Trials and Temptations: Tests of our faith produce maturity, humility, and patience.
    - Show Faith by Works- be doers not just hearers of the word.
    - Obedience to God's Word- leads to blessing.
    - Wisdom
    - Avoid Conflict, Love One Another
    - Tame/Control the Tongue, Honest Speech.
    - Humility- even believers stumble.
    - Dangers of Worldliness- avoid hypocrisy, resist the devil.
    - Money- the Christian's relationship with wealth
    - Patient Endurance, especially as we wait for Christ's return.
    - The Power of Prayer
    - God is in Control, Seek His Will

Note:
- Paul called James one of the pillars of the church (Galatians 2:9).
- James led the Jerusalem Council of AD 49/50.
- James was martyred for his faith. According to Hegesippus, James was pushed off the Temple pinnacle, then beaten with a club. Most scholars believe Jewish historian Josephus' version- James was stoned to death in AD 62.
- James in Hebrew is 'Jacob'.

You adulterous people, don't you know that friendship with the world means enmity against God? Anyone who chooses to be a friend of the world becomes an enemy of God.
James 4:4 NIV

KEY Verses:
- 1:2-4
- 1:12-15
- 1:19-22
- 2:12-13
- 2:18-19
- 3:6, 8-10
- 3:16-17
- 4:4, 7-10
- 4:14-15
- 5:7-12
- 5:16

Theme: Our faith must be made visible through our deeds.

1 PETER

Literary Style: Universal/General Epistle (letter)

New Testament Book # **21** | # of chapters **5**

Author — Peter, apostle of Jesus Christ dictated this letter to Silvanus (Silas) chapter 5:12-13, a Greek-speaking apostle. Peter, an uneducated fisherman spoke Aramaic and Hebrew, and knew basic Greek.

Audience — This letter, written in formal Greek, was meant to be circulated among the chosen- Jewish Christians living as exiles abroad in Pontus, Galatia, Cappadocia, Asia, and Bithynia.

Setting — Probably written in Rome between AD 64-68, during Nero's persecution of the Christian church. Mark was with Peter in Rome in the mid AD 60's (2 Timothy 4:11).

Of Interest — Jewish Christians had fled persecution in AD 66, after a Jewish uprising in Jerusalem resulted in the death of many Roman soldiers. Hatred of the Jews escalated following this rebellion.

General Information about the book of 1 PETER:

- Peter refers to Rome as Babylon, an Old Testament reference to corrupt and evil nations. Scholars believe he used the word Babylon instead of Rome as code word (or euphemism) to avoid angering Roman officials. His Jewish readers would understand this reference as 'all those who oppose God's people'.

Content Highlights:

- Peter begins with a poem – believers have hope in Christ despite their circumstances.
- Suffering builds faith, purifies believers.
- Obedience, we must live lives of holiness using Christ as our example.
- Believers are chosen by God, set apart – are given a new identity as brothers and sisters in Christ.
- Be an example to non-believers.
- Submit to authority.
- Behavior and conduct within Christian households
- Blessing through suffering.
- Love and serve others.
- Advice to the church elders.
- Resist evil, stand firm in the faith.

Note:
- Peter's name was Simeon Bar-Jonah, (son of Jonah John 1:42, Acts 15:14) though he is better known as Simon or Simon Peter.
- After Peter realized Jesus was the promised Messiah Jesus gave Simeon a nickname – *the Rock*, which is Cephas in Aramaic, Petra in Greek.
- Jesus commissioned Peter to take care of his sheep (the church, believers).

However, if you suffer as a Christian, do not be ashamed, but praise God that you bear that name.
1 Peter 4:16 NIV

KEY Verses:
- 1:2
- 1:5-7
- 1:14-19
- 1:23-25
- 2:2
- 2:9-10
- 2:11-12
- 2:21-23
- 2:24
- 3:3-4
- 3:8-9
- 3:17
- 3:18-19
- 4:2, 5-6
- 5:1-10

Theme: Encouragement and endurance despite persecution and trials.

2 PETER

Literary Style: Universal/General Epistle (letter)

New Testament Book #: 22 | # of chapters: 3

Author: Simeon Peter, apostle of Jesus, though no all biblical scholars agree (see below). Peter was in the inner circle of Christ's disciples (with James and John).

Audience: This letter is addressed to believers, probably the same group as First Peter.

Setting: Widely believed to have been written shortly after First Peter (mentioned in 3:1), between AD 64-68, during Nero's persecution of Christians and near the end of Peter's life.

Of Interest: Peter died as a martyr under Emperor Nero around AD 67-68. Nero died June 9 AD 68, at age 30.

General Information about the book of 2 PETER:
- This letter is Peter's farewell to the church. He mentions his imminent death and wrote this letter so the church would have a written record of his teachings.
- Some scholars question whether it was written by Peter for two reasons:
    1. Peter mentions Paul's letters at the conclusion of this book. These scholars do not think Paul's letters would be widely known until much later. In fact, the Thessalonian letters had been written in AD 50-51 and could have been widely circulated by AD 64. Peter mentions Paul's letters not in a compilation or formal collection, just that they exist, and that the church was familiar with them.
    2. The Greek used in this letter is informal, unlike the formal Greek in First Peter, and the writing style differs. It is thought that Peter dictated his first letter to Silvanus and wrote this second epistle himself.

Content Highlights:
- Peter calls on the believers to live holy, blameless lives.
- Peter assures the readers that his writings are true, he was an eyewitness to Jesus' ministry.
- The divine inspiration of Scripture.
- Warning against heresy and false teachers.
- Watch and be ready for Jesus' return.

The Lord is not slow in keeping his promise, as some understand slowness. Instead he is patient with you, not wanting anyone to perish, but everyone to come to repentance.
2 Peter 3:9 NIV

Note:
- Peter and his brother Andrew were fishermen from the town of Bethsaida.
- Peter was married, and Jesus had healed his mother-in-law of a fever (see Luke 4:38-39).
- Peter is the disciple who denied Jesus three times following Christ's arrest in Gethsemane.

KEY Verses:
- 1:3
- 1:20-21
- 2:18-21
- 3:3-7
- 3:9
- 3:10-13

Theme: Be watchful, remain true to God's word and avoid false teachings.

1 JOHN

Literary Style: Universal/General Epistle (letter)

New Testament Book # 23   # of chapters 5

Author: John, the 'beloved' disciple of Jesus. It is written in a similar style as John's gospel, and both Polycarp (an associate of John) and Irenaeus, Polycarp's student attributed it to John.

Audience: John has a fatherly concern for his readers, this letter is addressed to 'my little children'. John wrote to all Christians, he specifically addresses children, fathers and young men (2:12-14).

Setting: Estimates range from AD 60-100, it was probably written between AD 86-95, after his gospel and before his Revelation.

Of Interest: Gnostics believe that matter is evil, so God could not have created the universe. They deny that Jesus became a human.

General Information about the book of First John:
- This book was written:
    1. To warn believers of an emerging heresy, known today as Gnosticism.
    2. To assure Christians that they have eternal life through Christ.
- This book begins in a similar manner as John's gospel, referring to the *logos* (word) of God.

Content Highlights:
- Prologue
    - God is the source of life.
- God is Light
    - Believers must resist and confess sin, seek to walk in the light of righteousness.
    - Keep Gods commands and love one another.
    - Beware of the antichrist, avoid worldly temptations.
- God is Love
    - Love one another.
    - God lives within believers, enabling them to love each other perfectly, as God loves.
- Test the spirits to discern false prophets from truth.
- Be confident of eternal life.

> *He who has the Son has life; he who does not have the Son of God does not have life.*
> 1 John 5:12 NIV

Note:
- It is believed John was an old man when he wrote this book.
- John wrote five of the books included in the New Testament, second to Paul who wrote thirteen.

KEY Verses:
- 1:5 to 2:2
- 2:3-6
- 2:15-17
- 2:23
- 2:29
- 3:10
- 3:18
- 23-24
- 4:1-3
- 4:7-13
- 5:1-4
- 5:18

Theme: Jesus was fully human yet completely divine. Salvation and eternal life is only through belief in Him.

2 JOHN

Literary Style: Epistle (letter)

New Testament Book #: 24
# of chapters: 1

Author: The author is not identified by name. Written by "the elder", widely believed to be a pseudonym for the apostle John, who was also writing in his old age.

Audience: This letter is addressed to the "elect lady and her children", meaning the church. During this time of persecution, this is a way of mentioning the church without endangering specific individuals.

Setting: Estimates range from AD 70-100, most agree it was written between AD 85-95, after his gospel and before his Revelation. Many believe it was written from Ephesus where John lived in his later years.

Of Interest: The apostle Peter referred to himself as 'the elder' in his first letter.

General Information about the book of Second John:
- Written to encourage believers to continue in the faith.
- Warns against false teachers and false doctrine, specifically those mentioned in First John, the Gnostics.

Content Highlights:
- John's love for the church.
- John's delight in knowing the church is faithful and obedient.
- John's concern for the church. He warns against deception by false teachers.
- Knowledge and acceptance of Jesus as the Christ is a mark of true faith.
- In John's farewell, he states that he has more to say, but desires to visit with the church to communicate this information with them in person.

Who was John writing to?
- Some scholars believe John was writing literally to a specific woman and her children (instead of figuratively to 'the church' at large –see above). While they believe the greeting 'elect lady' is a reference to a given name, it should be noted that Elekta was not used as a personal name, and Kyria was used only rarely. The word *Eklekte* means 'elect' or 'chosen', and Kyria means 'lady,' 'mistress', or 'one who is in position of authority'.
- The word *Kuria*, (lady, mistress) is the Greek equivalent of Martha, some scholars believe John was writing to a woman named Martha, though there is no evidence of this.

And this is love: that we walk in obedience to his commands. As you have heard from the beginning, his command is that you walk in love.
2 John 1:6 NIV

KEY Verses
- 1:3
- 1:6
- 1:7
- 1:9-11

Theme: Show love to others using discernment and caution.

3 JOHN

Literary Style: Epistle (letter)

New Testament Book #: 25
# of chapters: 1

Author: Once again, the apostle John refers to himself as "the elder".

Audience: This letter is addressed to a Christian named Gaius; whom John calls his 'dear friend'.

Setting: Probably written between AD 80-95, while John was leading the church in Ephesus. The Temple in Jerusalem had been destroyed in AD 70, and Christians were scattered.

Of Interest: 2 and 3 John are referred to as the 'twin epistles' as they have similarities.

General Information about the book of Third John:

- This letter is written in response to reports John has received about two men in the church, Diotrephes and Demetrius. John wrote a letter to Diotrephes which was disregarded (1:9).

Content Highlights:

- John greets Gaius as a dear friend.
- He commends Gaius for his faithfulness to the truth, and hospitality towards visiting teachers.
- He encourages him to continue to support and welcome believers who remain true to the faith.
- John exposes Diotrephes slander against the truth, and his wrongful actions within the church community. Diotrephes rejected the teachers sent by John as well as other faithful Christians, whom he should have welcomed.
- John warns Gaius to avoid people like Diotrephes, but to surround himself with true believers such as Demetrius.
- He ends this letter in the same manner as 2 John- he has much more to say but wishes to do so in person.

Note:
- Many believe John wrote this letter while exiled on the Island of Patmos, Greece. He had been sent there under Roman Emperor Domitian.
- A temple to Domitian was built in Ephesus around AD 86, and the people were forced to worship and make sacrifices to Domitian- something John would have denounced. He was exiled to the island around AD 94.

Dear friend, do not imitate what is evil but what is good. Anyone who does what is good is from God. Anyone who does what is evil has not seen God.
3 John 1:11, NIV

KEY Verses:
- 1:4
- 1:8
- 1:11

Theme: Avoid what is evil, teach and cling to the truth.

JUDE

Literary Style: General/Universal Epistle (letter)

New Testament Book # 26
# of chapters 1

Author: Jude, the brother of James who were both brothers to Jesus (Mark 5:3). Like James, Jude misunderstood Jesus' teaching and did not believe he was the Messiah until later in life (John 7:5).

Audience: This letter is addressed to Christians- 'the called, loved by God the Father and kept for Jesus Christ" (verse 1b).

Setting: Probably written between AD 65-80.

Of Interest: Jude became a leader in the Jerusalem church shortly after Jesus' resurrection (Acts 1:14).

General Information about the book of JUDE:
- Peter's second epistle contains many similar words and phrases as Jude (see 2 Peter 2:1-18).
- In his letter, Jude references apocryphal texts including the Book of 1 Enoch (vs. 9) and the Assumption of Moses.

Content Highlights:
- Jude begins by revealing that he originally intended to write about salvation but felt it necessary to address more pressing issues within the church.
- Ungodly men, ruled by their passions were using God's grace as a license to sin. They denied Jesus was God and refused to submit to His divine authority.
- Jude uses biblical examples to remind his readers of God's judgement upon the wicked.
- He urges his readers not to be led astray, to remain faithful and to pray in the Holy Spirit. To fight against this attack, showing mercy to those who have been deceived lest they also suffer eternal punishment.

But you, dear friends, by building yourselves up in your most holy faith and praying in the Holy Spirit, keep yourselves in God's love as you wait for the mercy of our Lord Jesus Christ to bring you to eternal life.
Jude 1:20-21 NIV

Note:
- The name Jude is short for *Judah* in Hebrew and *Judas* in Greek. It was a common name in Palestine.
- Jude's closing, or benediction is considered by many to be one of the most beautiful in the entire bible (1:24-25).

KEY Verses:
- 1:3-5
- 1:10
- 1:17-19
- 1:20-21

Theme: Defend the truth, showing mercy and love to others.

REVELATION

Literary Style: Apocalyptic Prophecy

New Testament Book #: 27
# of chapters: 22

Author > The apostle John, the 'beloved disciple'. It is likely he was the last remaining of Jesus' 12 disciples. John was given a vision and was commanded to write what he saw on a scroll

Audience > This letter is a circular letter, originally sent to the seven churches located in Asia Minor- Ephesus, Smyrna, Pergamum, Thyatira, Sardis, Philadelphia, and Laodicea.

Setting > Believed by many to have been written at the end of John's life, while he was a prisoner on Patmos, around AD 95-96 (1:9).

Of Interest > Patmos housed a temple to Artemis, an acropolis, administrative center, and a hippodrome. Prisoners were forced to work in the mines located on the island.

General Information about the book of REVELATION:
- A revelation is the unveiling of something that was previously hidden. In this book John reveals what will occur in the last days and at Jesus' second coming.
- John wrote to the seven churches, addressing issues pertaining to each one individually. These included doctrinal error, corruption, and persecution.
- Much of this book is symbolic, and various interpretations are debated among believers.

Content Highlights:
- Prologue and letters to the seven churches.
- He is given a glimpse into the Throne Room of Heaven and of future events:
  - the scroll with seven seals, and the opening of these seals.
  - The seven trumpets
  - The two witnesses
  - The woman, the child, and the dragon
  - The beast from the sea, the beast from the earth
  - The seven bowl judgements
  - The fall of Babylon
  - The four horsemen of the apocalypse
  - The thousand-year reign, release of Satan
  - The Great White Throne judgement
  - New heaven and new earth.

Note > John outlived all the other apostles. His brother, James was the first apostle martyred. It is unknown whether John died on Patmos or was freed prior to his death. It is possible Domitian's successor, Nerva released John from Patmos in AD 96.

> The seventh angel sounded his trumpet, and there were loud voices in heaven, which said: "The kingdom of the world has become the kingdom of our Lord and of his Messiah, and he will reign for ever and ever."
> Revelation 11:13 NIV

KEY Verses
- 1:3
- 1:8
- 3:19-20
- 5:2-5
- 5:13-14
- 7:13-17
- 11:15-18
- 12:1-3
- 13:11-18
- 14:6-13
- 15:3-4
- 17:14
- 19:7-9
- 20:15
- 21:22-27
- 22:16-20

Theme > Jesus has conquered sin and death; He will reward those who believe in Him with eternal life.

Wildrose Media website
Home Page

Faith Family Fun Blog

Wildrose Media website
Shop Page

Additional books from Wildrose Media, available on Amazon:

Sermon Notebook
Kids Ages 9-12 years
Cross cover

Sermon Notebook
Kids Ages 6-8 years
Bunny cover

The Birth of Jesus
Coloring Book

The Story of Easter
Coloring Book
Blue cover

Bible Teaching Sheets
Old Testament - KJV

Bible Teaching Sheets
New Testament - KJV

Friendship and Freedom
Story of the Statue of Liberty

100 Questions to Ask Myself
Vol.1 - pink cover

Ultimate Fishing Journal
for Kids Vol. 1

Ultimate Fishing Journal
for Girls - pink cover

Headache Diary, 5"x 6"
Symptom Notebook

Dutch Boy & Girl
Small Notebook 5"x6"

The above book QR codes are Amazon Affiliate links,
I may receive compensation from purchases made using these links,
at no additional cost to you.

Made in United States
Troutdale, OR
03/04/2025